A New True Book

TELEVISION

By Karen Jacobsen

*This "true book" was prepared
under the direction of
Illa Podendorf,
formerly with the Laboratory School,
University of Chicago*

CP CHILDRENS PRESS, CHICAGO

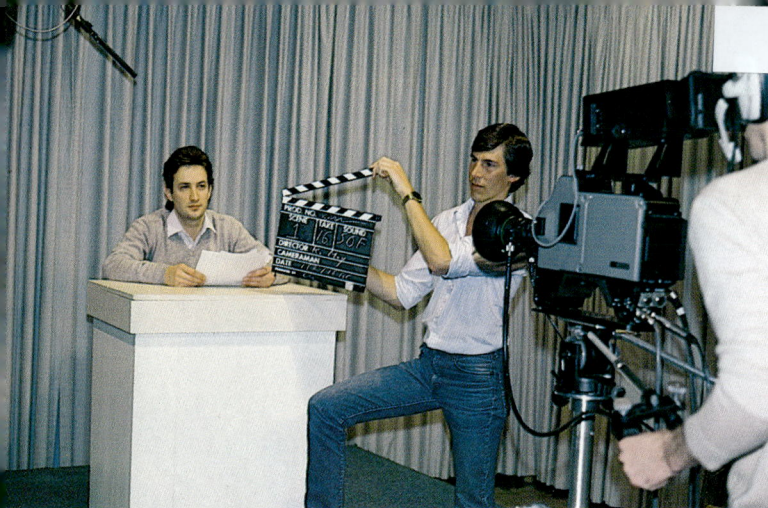

Stagehand with clap board

PHOTO CREDITS

Ken May—2, 22 (3 photos), 26 (2 photos), 43

Photos Courtesy of WGN Television, Chicago—20 (right), 44 (top)

Tony Romano—Cover, 4, 20 (left), 44 (bottom)

UPI Photo—42

RCA—13, 14, 15 (2 photos), 16, 41

Jon Randolp, WTTW—19 (2 photos), 21, 23, 25, (3 photos), 27, 29, 31, 32, 37, 38, 39

John Forsberg—7, 8, 10, 11, 35

COVER—A television broadcast

Library of Congress Cataloging in Publication Data

Jacobsen, Karen.
  Television.

  (A New true book)
  Includes index.
  Summary: Explains in simple terms how
television works, the history of its invention,
and how television programs are made.
  1. Television—Juvenile literature.
[1. Television] I. Title.
TK6640.J33   621.388   82-4456
ISBN 0-516-01659-8____ AACR2

TABLE OF CONTENTS

HOW TELEVISION WORKS

Television starts with light.
A television camera "sees"
light through its lens.
Inside the camera mirrors
divide the light into three
colors: red, green, and
blue.

Then, each of the colors
is sent into a camera tube.
There is a tube for each
color.

COLOR CAMERA

Camera
Tubes

Light
Enters

Red
Signal

Green
Signal

Blue
Signal

Mirror System

Electron Beam

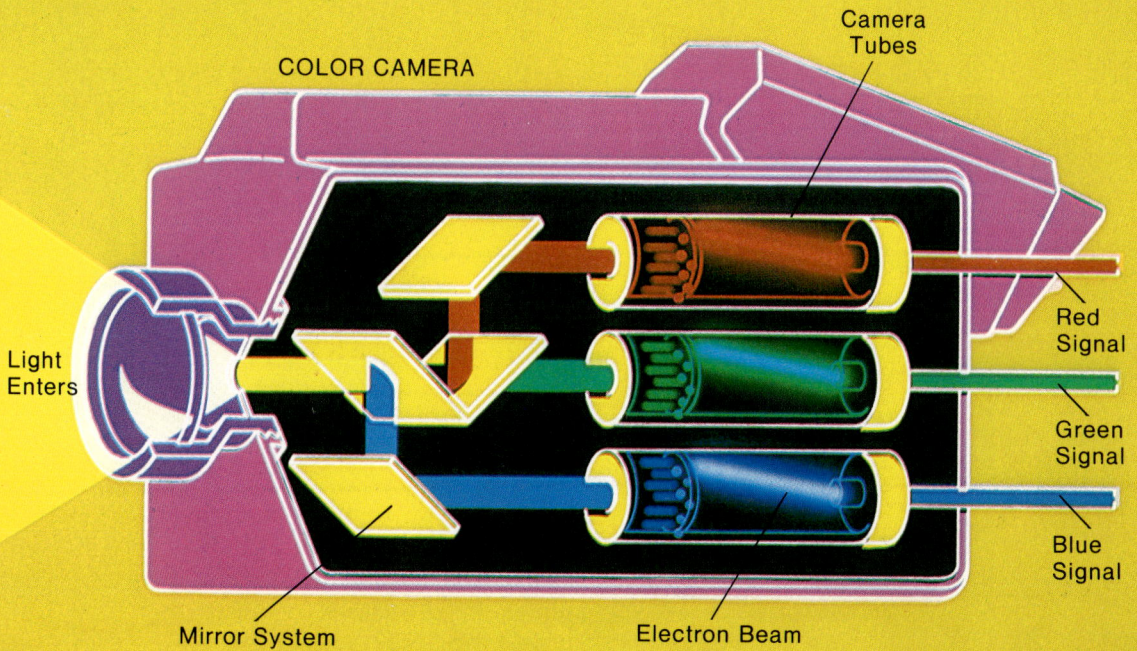

The camera tube
changes the light signal
into a color picture signal
and sends it out, as a red,
green, and blue signal.

Microphone

TV Signal

Amplifier

Antenna

Color Camera

Audio Signal

Encoder

Transmitter

Color Signals

Video Signal

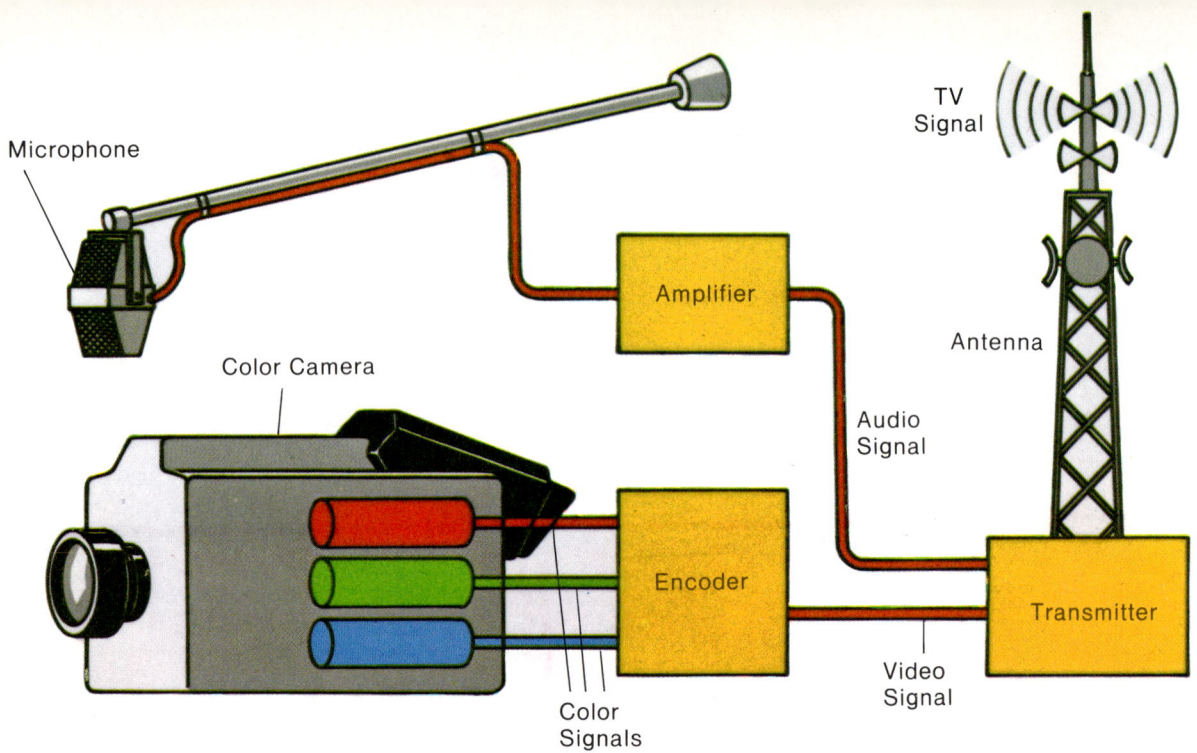

The three picture signals are put together and sent out as one strong picture signal.

A television program is part sound and part picture. Sound is called audio. The picture is called video.

A transmitter puts the sound and the picture together. It sends it out to an antenna.

The picture tube in your TV set "receives" this signal. It separates the one signal into parts again.

Each picture tube separates the color signal into three parts: red, green, and blue.

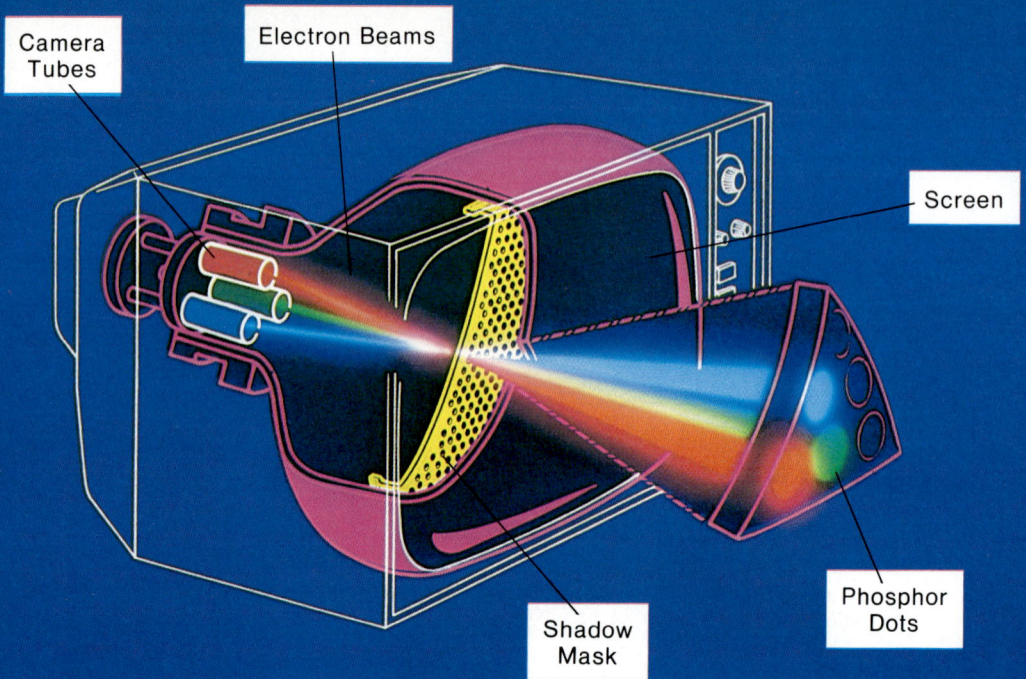

Camera Tubes

Electron Beams

Screen

Phosphor Dots

Shadow Mask

A TV screen is covered with thousands of tiny holes you can't see.

A second screen is coated with thousands of phosphor dots. (Phosphor is a chemical that glows when light strikes it.)

Decoder

Video
Signal

TV
Signal

Antenna

Amplifier

Audio
Signal

Picture
Tube

Speaker

Electronic
Circuits

Tuner

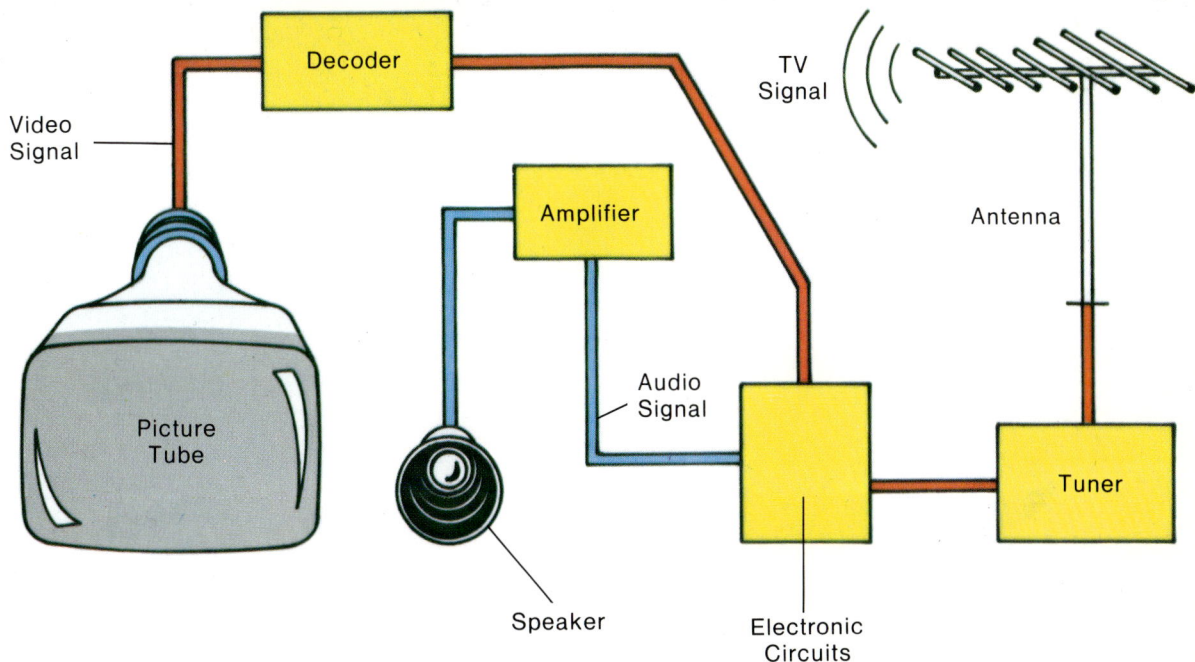

Each dot has three parts. The red part only lights up for a red electron, the green... for a green electron, and the blue... for a blue electron.

All of these tiny dots of light and color combine to make a picture.

11

THE FIRST TELEVISIONS

Television is a new invention. It is younger than radio, and radio is less than a hundred years old. People could listen to music, plays, sports, and news on radios. But people wanted to be able to hear and see these programs. People wanted television.

Television broadcast made in April, 1939 at the New York World's Fair. This was the first time a news event was ever covered by television.

Scientists set to work to find a way to send pictures along with the sound of radio.

Dr. Vladimir K. Zworykin invented the all-electronic "eye" of the television camera.

In 1929, the first black and white camera tube and picture tube were made by Vladimir K. Zworykin, a Russian-born American. The picture was small and not very clear, but it worked.

Scientists kept working.

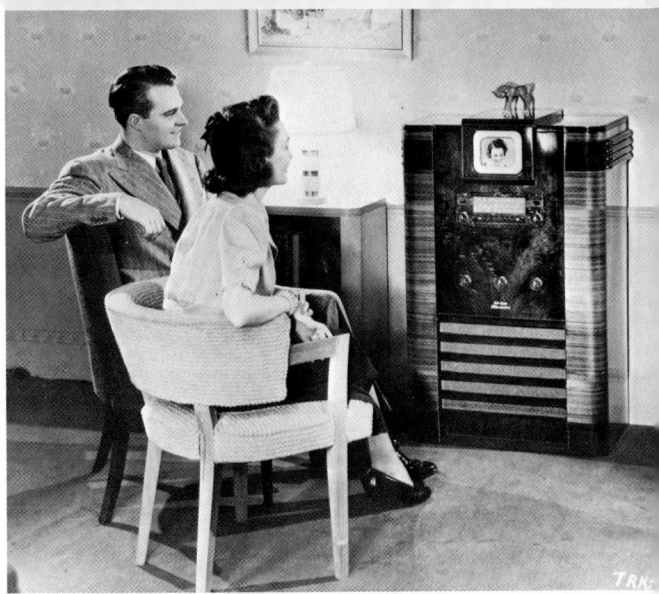

Above: 1939 black-and-white television
Left: In 1928 this picture of Felix the Cat
was sent from New York City to
Kansas as part of an experiment.

By 1936, there were television broadcasts only in New York City.

In 1939 at the New York World's Fair, millions of people saw television for the first time. They were amazed.

The first commercial color televisions were made by RCA in 1954.

Television became popular. But all the shows were in black and white. By 1953, there was color television.

Today television is everywhere. It can be seen on giant-sized screens or on tiny ones. Television shows you what you would see if you were there in person.

INSIDE A TELEVISION STUDIO

Most television programs are put together in a studio. A studio has no outside windows and very thick walls. It is designed to keep out unwanted light and sound.

A television studio is filled with special equipment. Dozens of powerful lights hang from its ceilings.

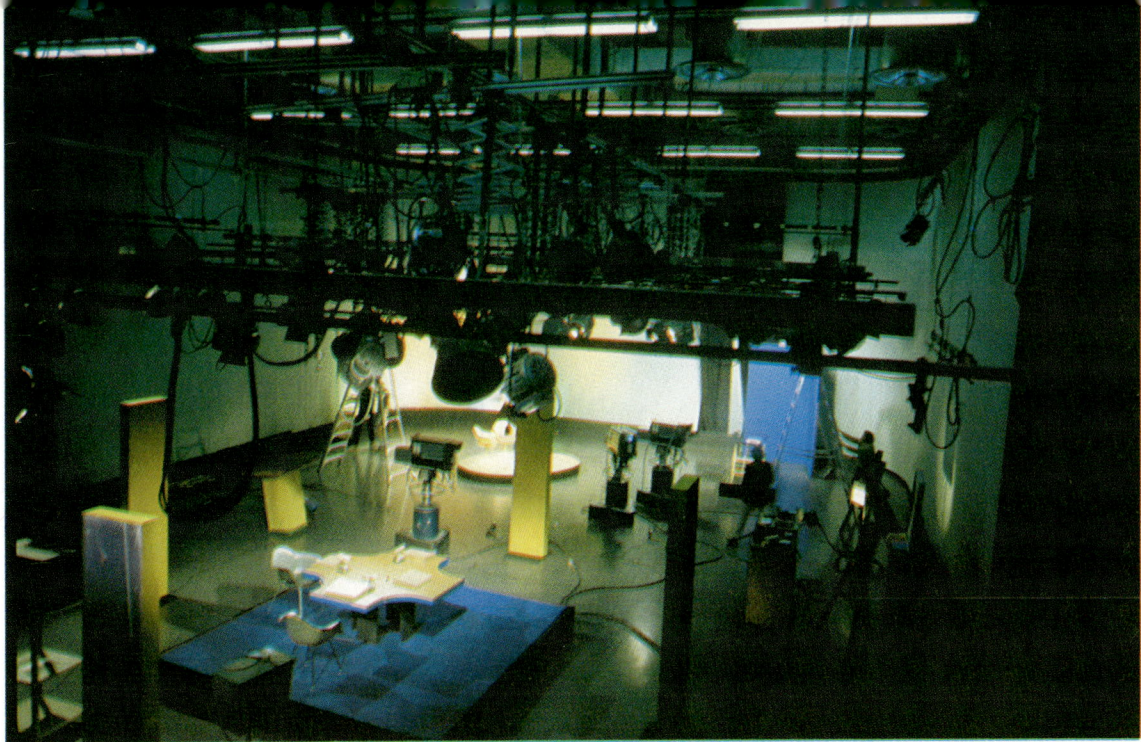

Television cameras can move from place to place.

It takes three or more cameras to cover the action of a television show. The cameras can move. They can tip up or down and turn around in a circle. A camera operator aims the camera. A helper

moves the camera's wires
and cables.

Sometimes a camera is
mounted on a crane. A
camera crane can move
high and low to get a
better look at what's
happening.

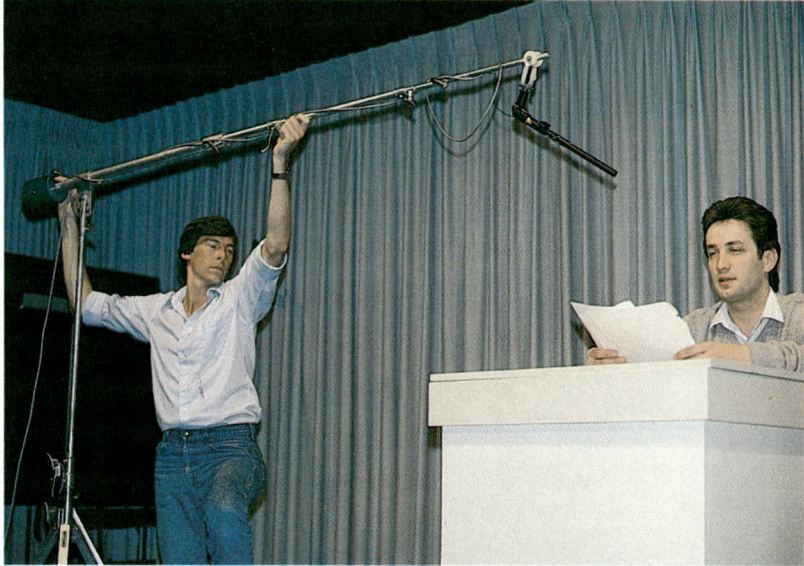

Right: Overhead microphone with boom
Below: Clip-on microphone
Below right: Hand held microphone

People use microphones
on television.

Near the studio is the control room. It is a very busy and important place. The people and equipment here control the sound and the picture that will be sent out.

THE PEOPLE WHO WORK IN TELEVISION

The people who appear in front of the cameras are called talent. They can be speakers, actors, musicians, dancers, reporters—anyone at all. If they appear on TV, then they are talent.

People in front of the cameras are important. But, it takes many other people to make a television show.

A floor manager uses hand signals to tell the talent when to speak and which camera to look at.

A cue card person holds up large cards with writing on them. The cards tell the talent what to say.

Below: Floor manager
Right: Cue card

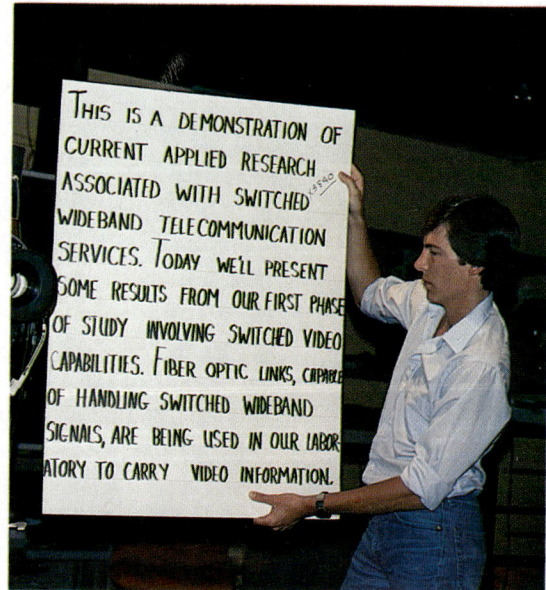

THIS IS A DEMONSTRATION OF CURRENT APPLIED RESEARCH ASSOCIATED WITH SWITCHED WIDEBAND TELECOMMUNICATION SERVICES. TODAY WE'LL PRESENT SOME RESULTS FROM OUR FIRST PHASE OF STUDY INVOLVING SWITCHED VIDEO CAPABILITIES. FIBER OPTIC LINKS, CAPABLE OF HANDLING SWITCHED WIDEBAND SIGNALS, ARE BEING USED IN OUR LABORATORY TO CARRY VIDEO INFORMATION.

Stagehands set up and remove scenery before, during, and after the show. They make sure everything is in its place.

Make-up and wardrobe people see to it that the talent look their best.

The director is in charge of the control room and the show. The director watches a row of television receivers. There is one receiver for each camera in the studio. The director decides which picture to use and when to change to another picture.

The director, technical director, and production assistant sit in the control room.

Sitting next to the director is the technical director. The T.D. helps the director. He makes the picture changes.

The production assistant watches the script to make sure nothing is left out.

The production assistant also keeps track of the time. The program must not be too long or too short.

Audio engineers watch
dials to make sure that the
sound coming from each
microphone is as loud and
clear as it should be.

Video engineers make sure that the picture coming from each camera is as bright and sharp as it can be.

TELEVISION TRANSMITTERS

The audio and the video travel from the control room to the master control room.

This room is full of equipment. Here the audio and the video are made stronger and sent to a transmitter.

A transmitter has to be as high as possible, so that its signals can go as far as possible.

Video signals can only travel about 50 or 60 miles from the transmitter. To go any farther, they need help.

Some signals are sent from one transmitter to another, and to another, and to another... and so on. They form a chain of transmitters to cover long distances.

Other signals are sent out into space, to a satellite. The satellite sends the video signal back to another place on earth.

TELEVISION TODAY

People can watch important events while they are happening.

News programs are usually live. They have one or more reporters.

News programs use film and videotape pictures to show the news. Film and videotape are recorded

before the program, in
another place.

Live shows need a lot of
teamwork. They can go
very well, but there is
always the chance that
something will go wrong.

Programs are pre-recorded on videotape. Videotape can be edited. A mistake can be cut out.

Sometimes performers can do their acts two or three times. Then the director can pick the best one to put into the show.

To show some events on television, the studio and control room must leave the studio. All of the equipment must be taken to the place where the event is being held. This is called "doing a remote broadcast."

Sports shows use a lot of special effects. A key play in a game can be shown over and over again (instant replay). The tape can be slowed down (slow motion) and stopped (stop action) at a special moment. The picture can even be split into 2 or 3

Special effects help people really see what's happening
at broadcasts made outside the studio.

sections. Each section can
show a different part of
the action.

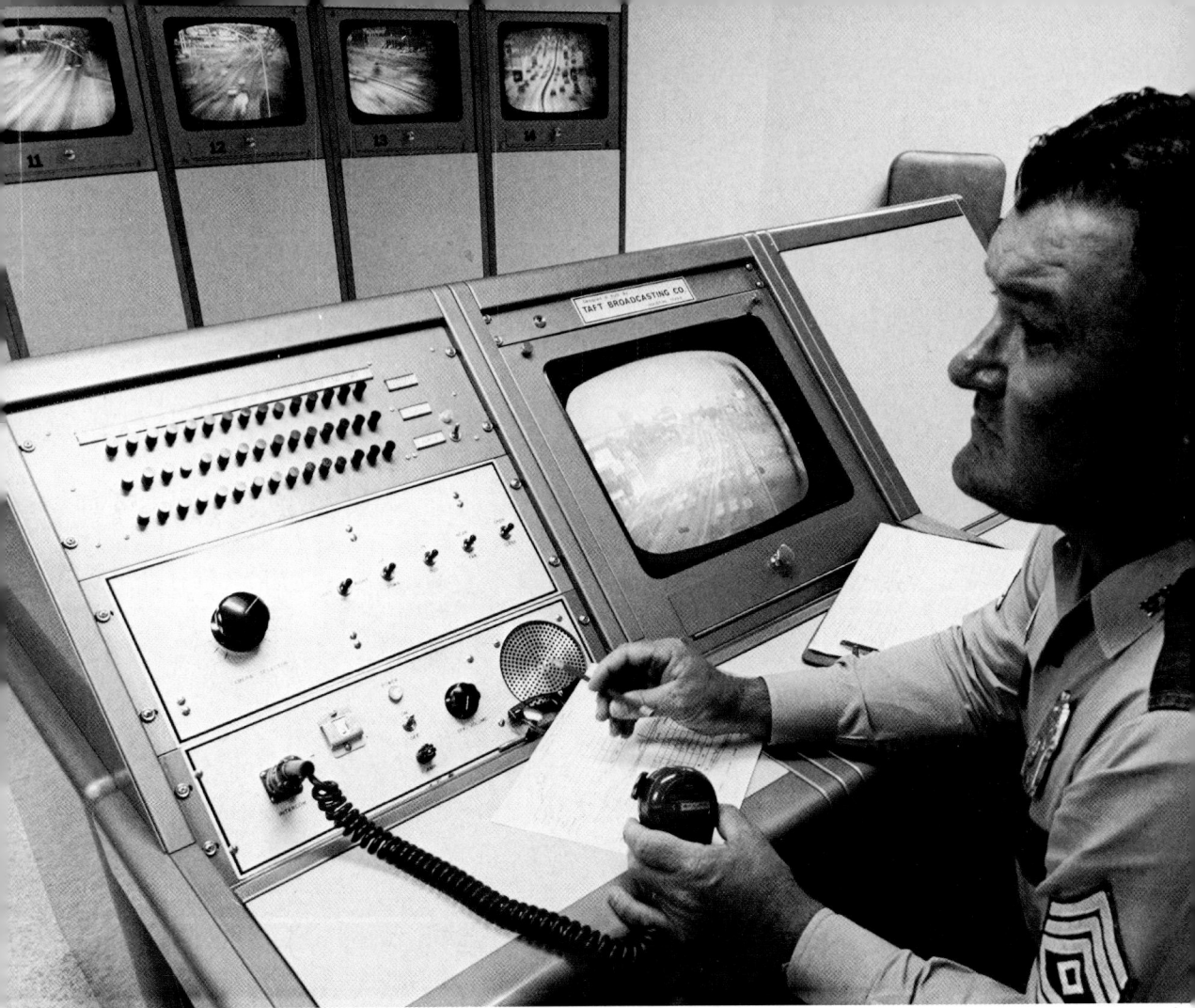

Television cameras serve
as guards. They are on
duty in banks, stores, and
many other places.

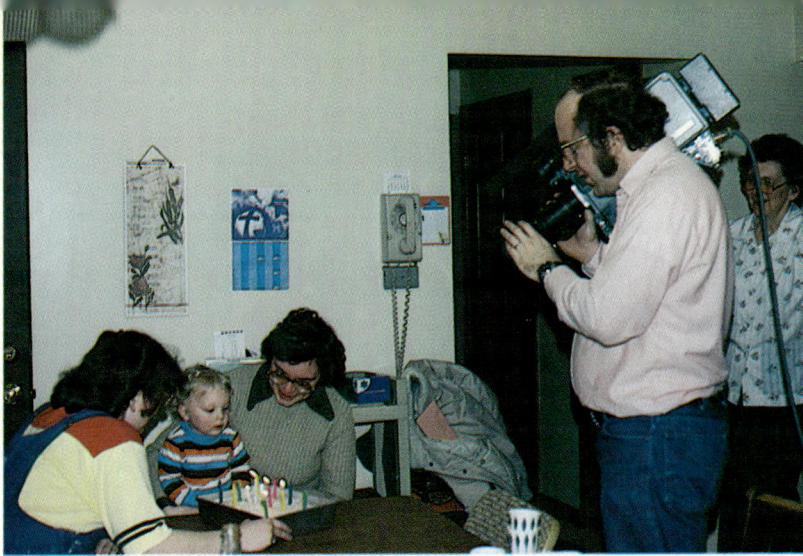

One person can watch many places. If something goes wrong, help can be sent right away.

Today, many people have their own television cameras and videotape recorders. They can make their own live television shows.

Television has become an important way to show and record events and information. It is used in schools, in businesses, and in the home.

Television can be exciting and entertaining. It can even be boring.

Television is always changing. There are new programs and new uses.

Television is an amazing invention. It is a part of everyone's life.

WORDS YOU SHOULD KNOW

amaze(ah • MAIZ) — to fill with surprise or wonder; astonish

assistant(ah • SIS • tent) — someone who helps

cable(KAY • bil) — a bundle of protected wires that carry an electric current

constant(KAHN • stent) — not changing; to stay the same

control room(kun • TROHL ROOM) — the place where the directions and commands come from

crane(KRAYN) — a machine that is used to move or lift heavy things

cue(KYOO) — words written for performers; reminders

designed(dih • ZINED) — planned for a special purpose

electron(ee • LEK • tron) — one of the smallest pieces of matter

entertain(en • ter • TANE) — to hold the attention of in a pleasant way; amuse

invention(in • VEN • shun) — an object that was made or created

manager(MAN • uh • jer) — a person who is in charge; director

mounted(MOUN • ted) — to put on top of

phosphor(FOSS • fer) — a chemical that glows when light strikes it

production(pro • DUK • shun) — the making and presentation of a movie, play, or other kind of entertainment

remote(re • MOTE) — to be away from the studio.

satellite(SAT • el • lite) — a man-made object that is put into space by a rocket and used to send television signals

script(SKRIPT) — the words spoken by talent

studio(STOO • dyo) — a place where television shows are made and broadcast

talent(TAL • ent) — people who appear on television

technical(TEK • nih • kil) — that part of television dealing with the pictures and sound that are broadcast

transmitter(TRANZ • mitter) — a device that sends out television signals

video(VID • ee • oh) — the part of a television broadcast that can be seen

videotape(VID • ee • oh • taip) — a special kind of magnetic recording tape used to record the picture and sound of a television program

visual(VIZJ • oo • al) — having to do with sight

wardrobe(WOR • drohb) — clothing

INDEX

About the Author

Karen Jacobsen is a graduate of the University of Connecticut and Syracuse University. She has been a teacher and is a writer. She likes to find out about interesting subjects and then write about them.